AltStrings Fiddle Method

FOR VIOLIN

Books 1 and 2

Piano Accompaniment for Violin
Original Key
Second Edition

Caroline McCaskey

Music Arranged by Caroline McCaskey

Cover Design: Mary Margaret McMurtry
www.marymcmurtrydesign.com

Cover Art and Illustrations: Jessica Blackburn, Blackburn Renderings
www.blackburnrenderings.com

Graphic Layout and Music Engraving: Charylu Roberts, O.Ruby Productions
www.selfpublishmusicbooks.com

·ALTSTRINGS·

ISBN 978-1-952077-02-9

AltStrings Fiddle Method

FOR VIOLIN

Book 1

Piano Accompaniment for Violin
Original Key

Second Edition

Table of Contents

Book 1 Songs

Twinkle, Twinkle Little Star

This intro part is not in the violin book,
but it may be played by either violin or piano, or both.

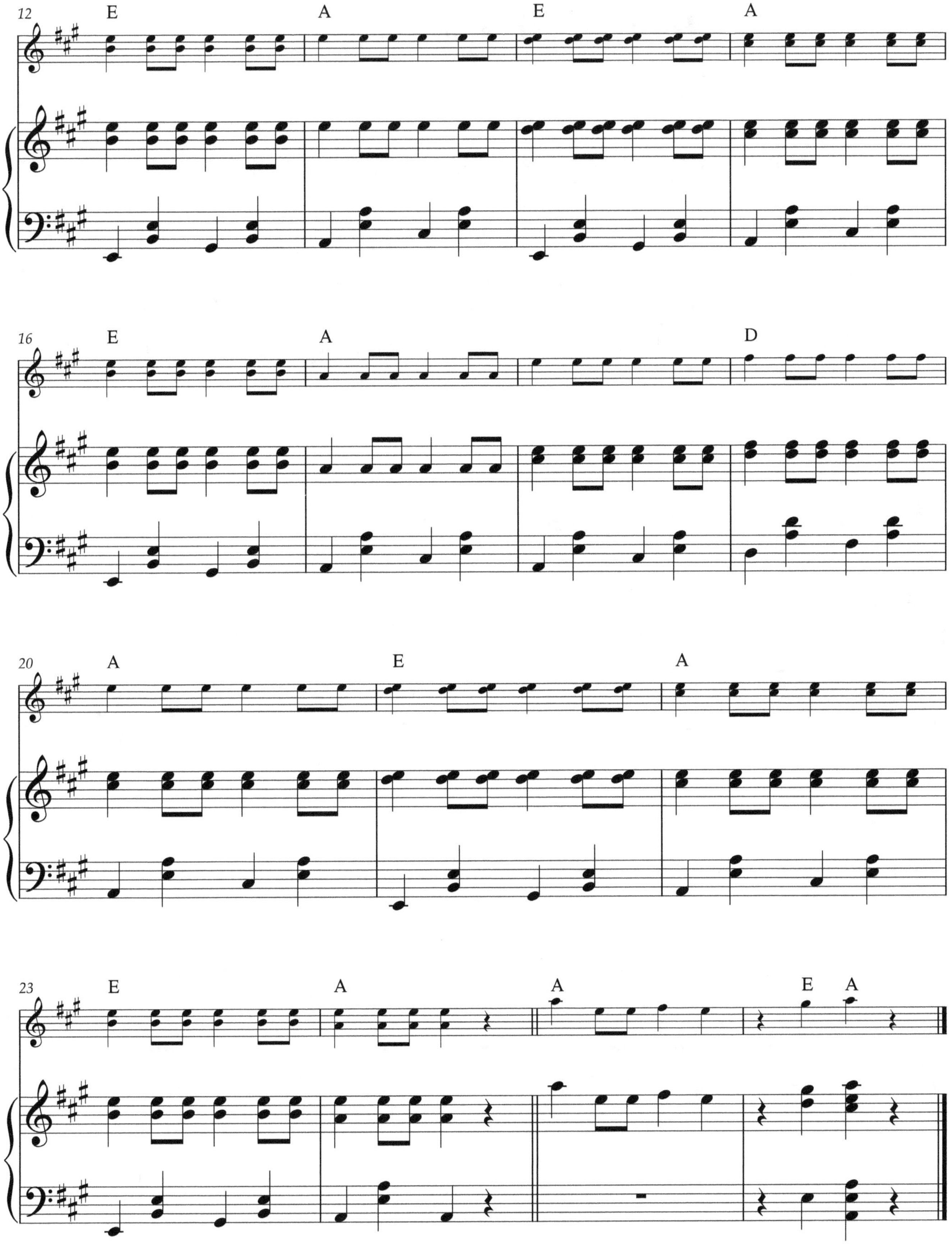
12
E
A
E
A
16
E
A
D
20
A
E
A
23
E
A
A
E
A

Mary Had a Little Lamb

Goodbye Liza Jane

7

Highland Laddie

Kerry Polka

Cripple Creek

Rubber Dolly

Moneymusk

Note: the string part repeats bars 5-8
instead of continuing on to bars 9-12.

Old Joe Clark

Peek-A-Boo Waltz

William J. Scanlan, 1856-1898

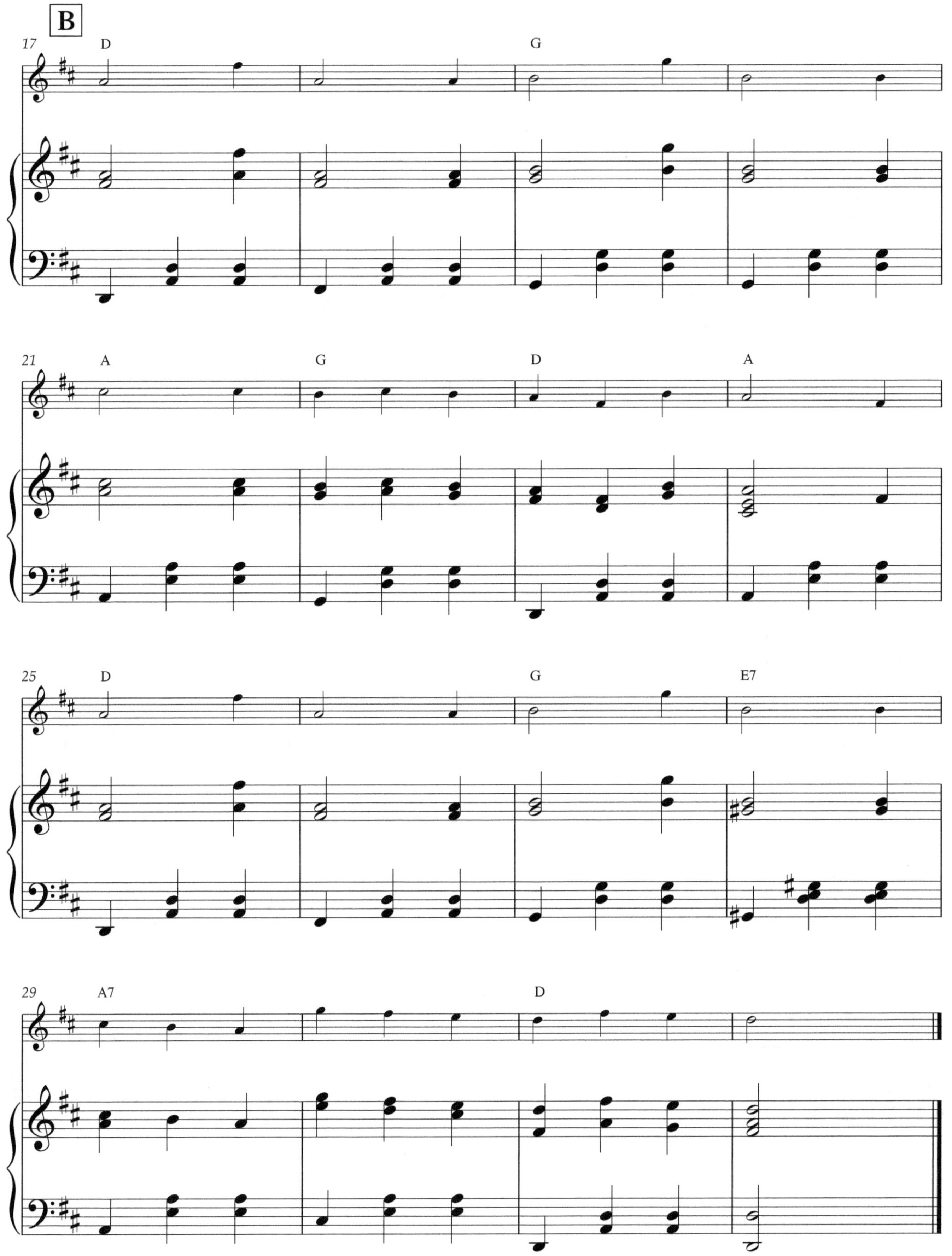
B
17
D
G
21
A
G
D
A
25
D
G
E7
29
A7
D

Cluck Old Hen

12 Skye Boat Song

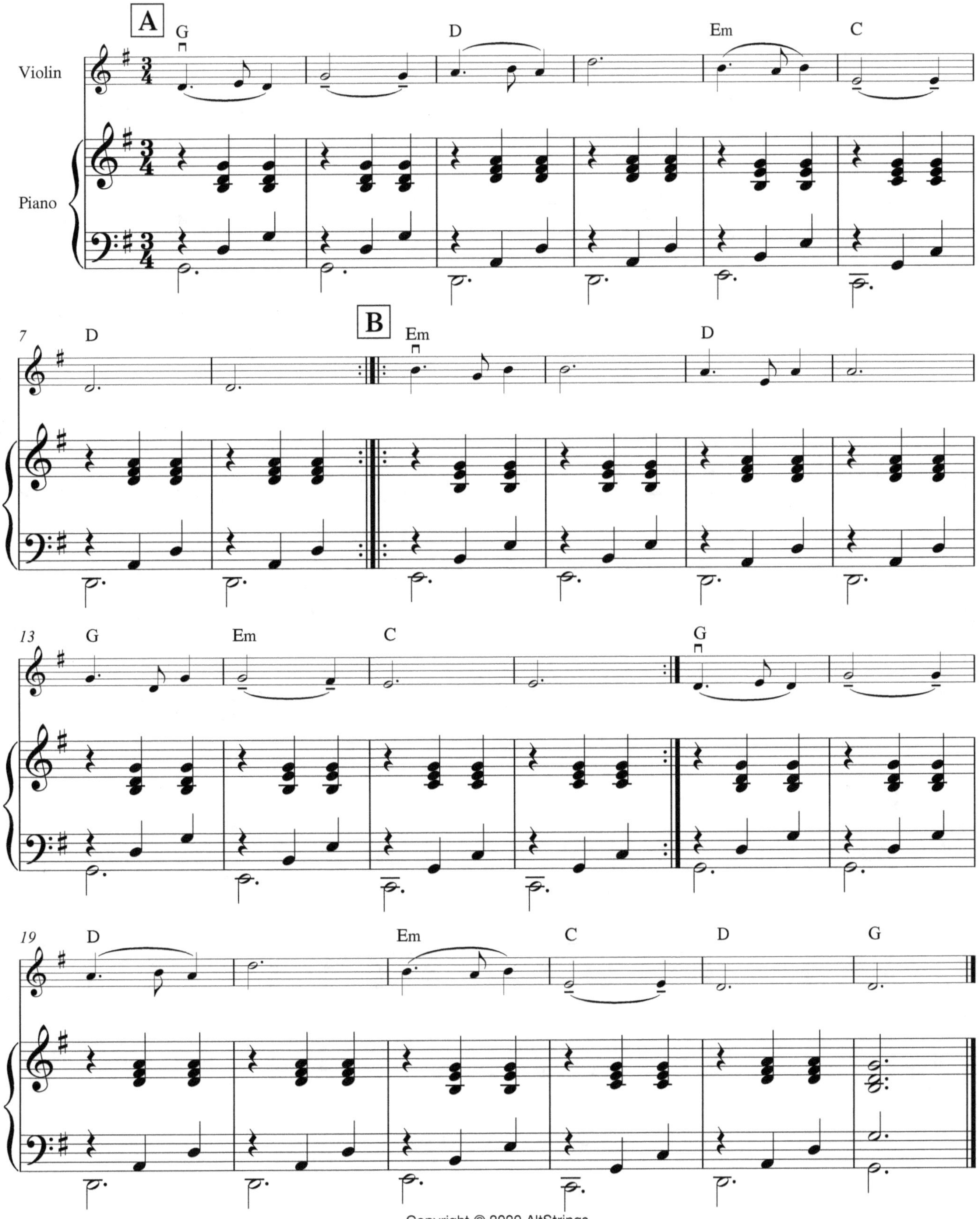

La Bastringue

Soldier's Joy

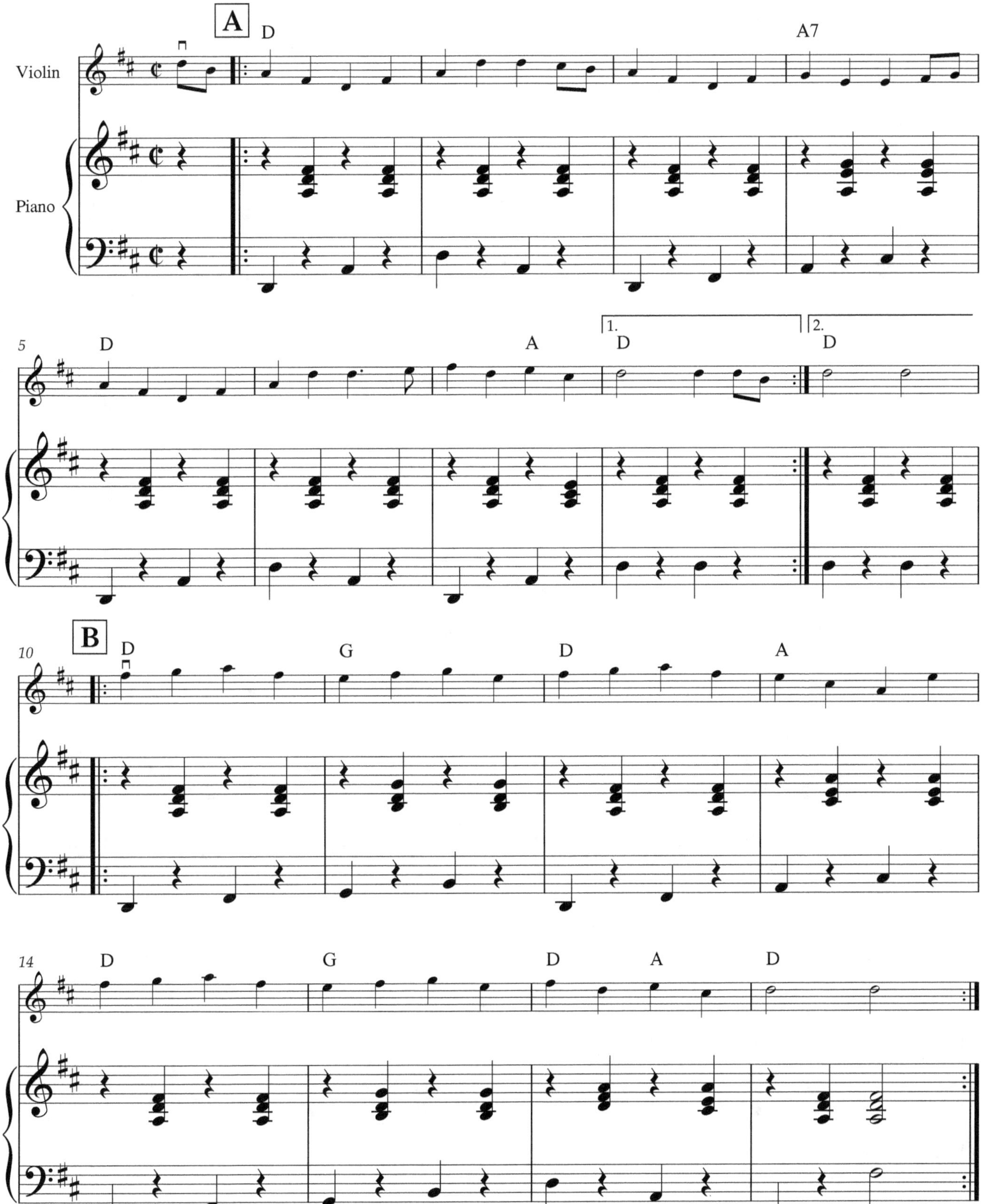

Sweet Betsy from Pike

Love Somebody

Red Haired Boy

22

Row Your Boat

Note: Violin part written as eight bars with a repeat

Pop Goes the Weasel

24

Off She Goes

AltStrings Fiddle Method

FOR VIOLIN

Book 2

Piano Accompaniment for Violin
Original Key

Second Edition

Table of Contents

Book 2 Songs

Chapel Hill Serenade

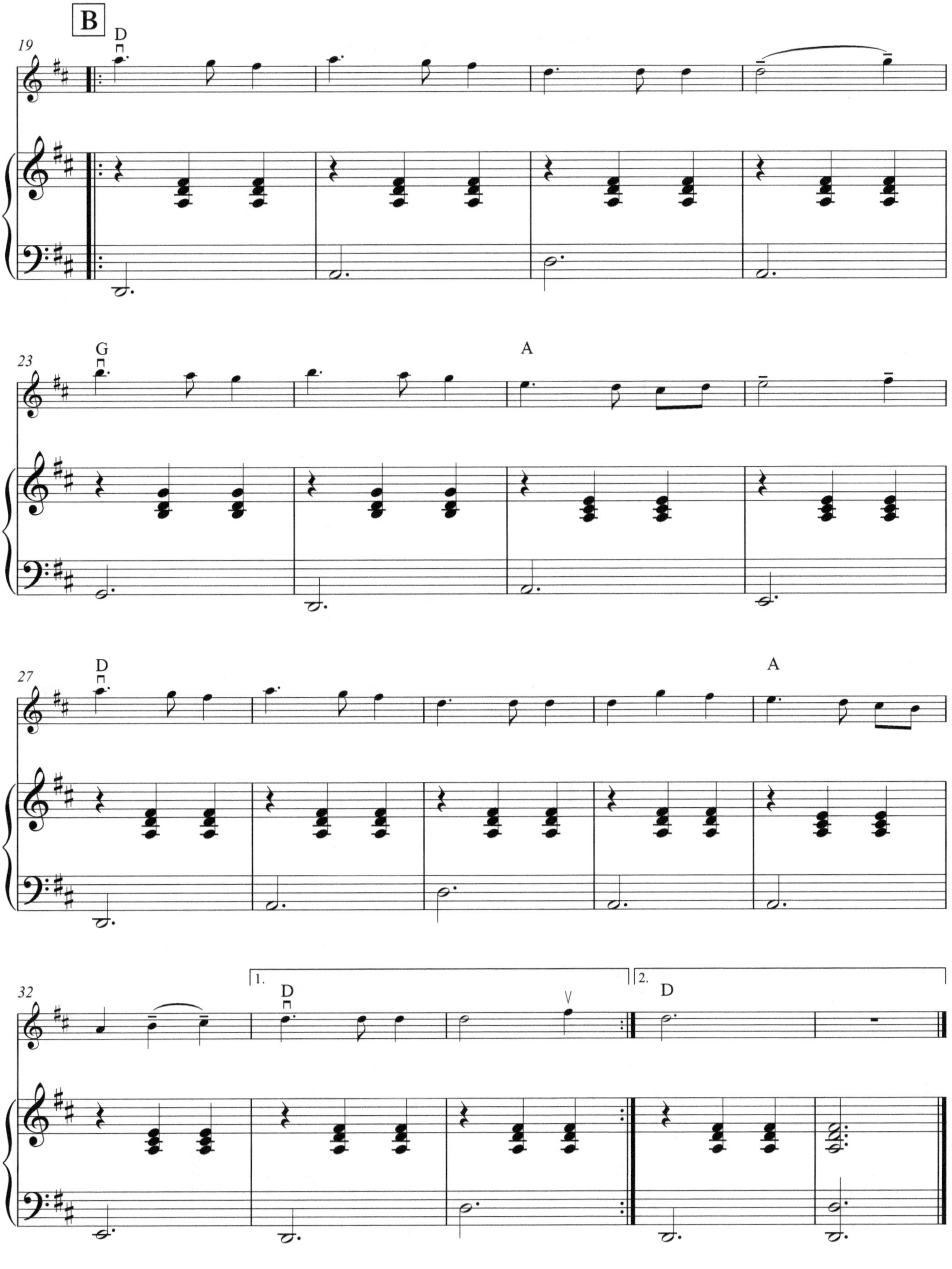
B
19
D
23
G
A
27
D
A
32
1.
D
2.
D

Crow Little Rooster

Atholl Highlanders

31

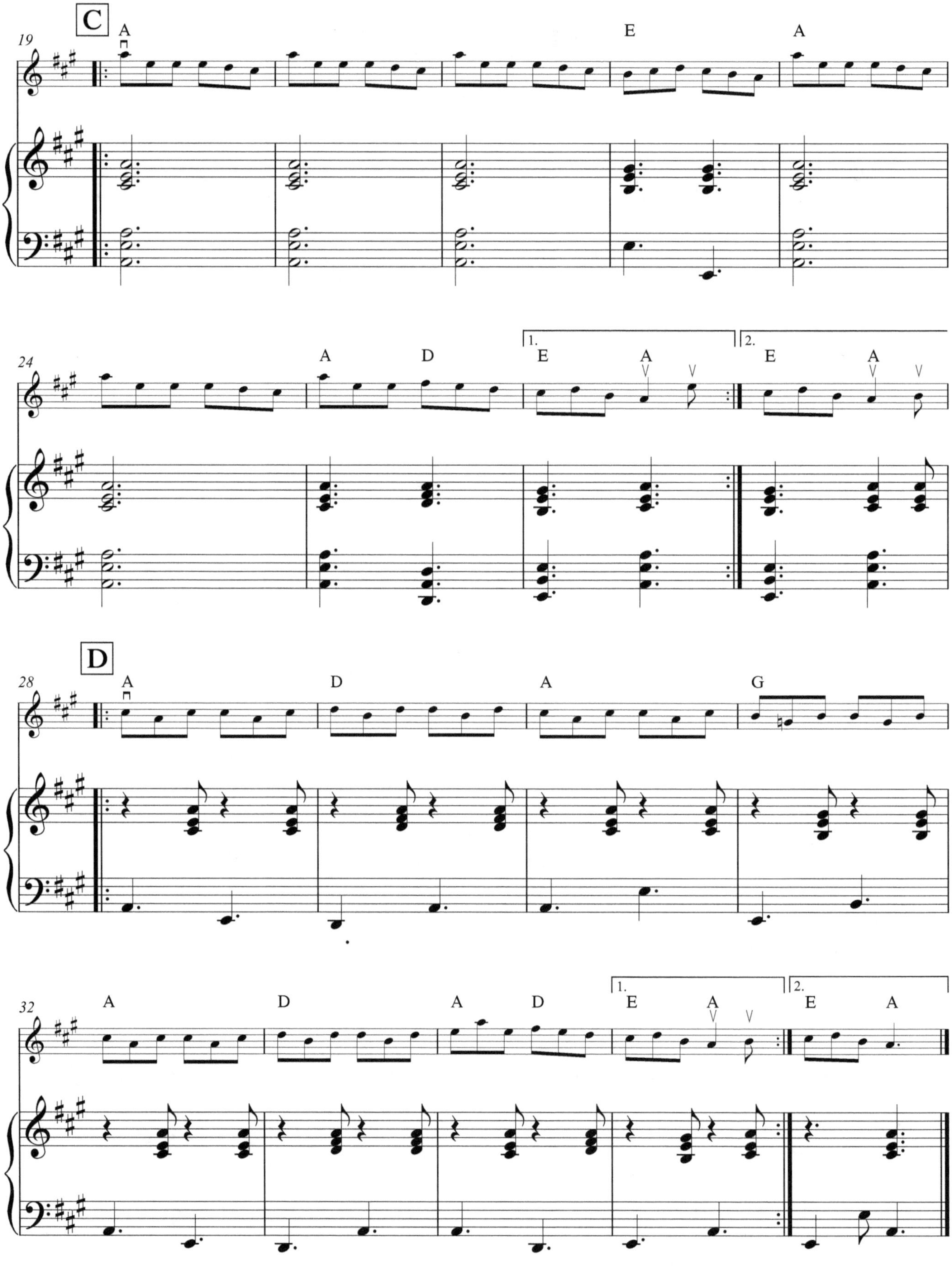
C
19
A E A
24
A D E A E A
1. 2.
D
28
A D A G
32
A D A D E A E A
1. 2.

John Ryan's Polka

33

Bonaparte Crossing the Rhine

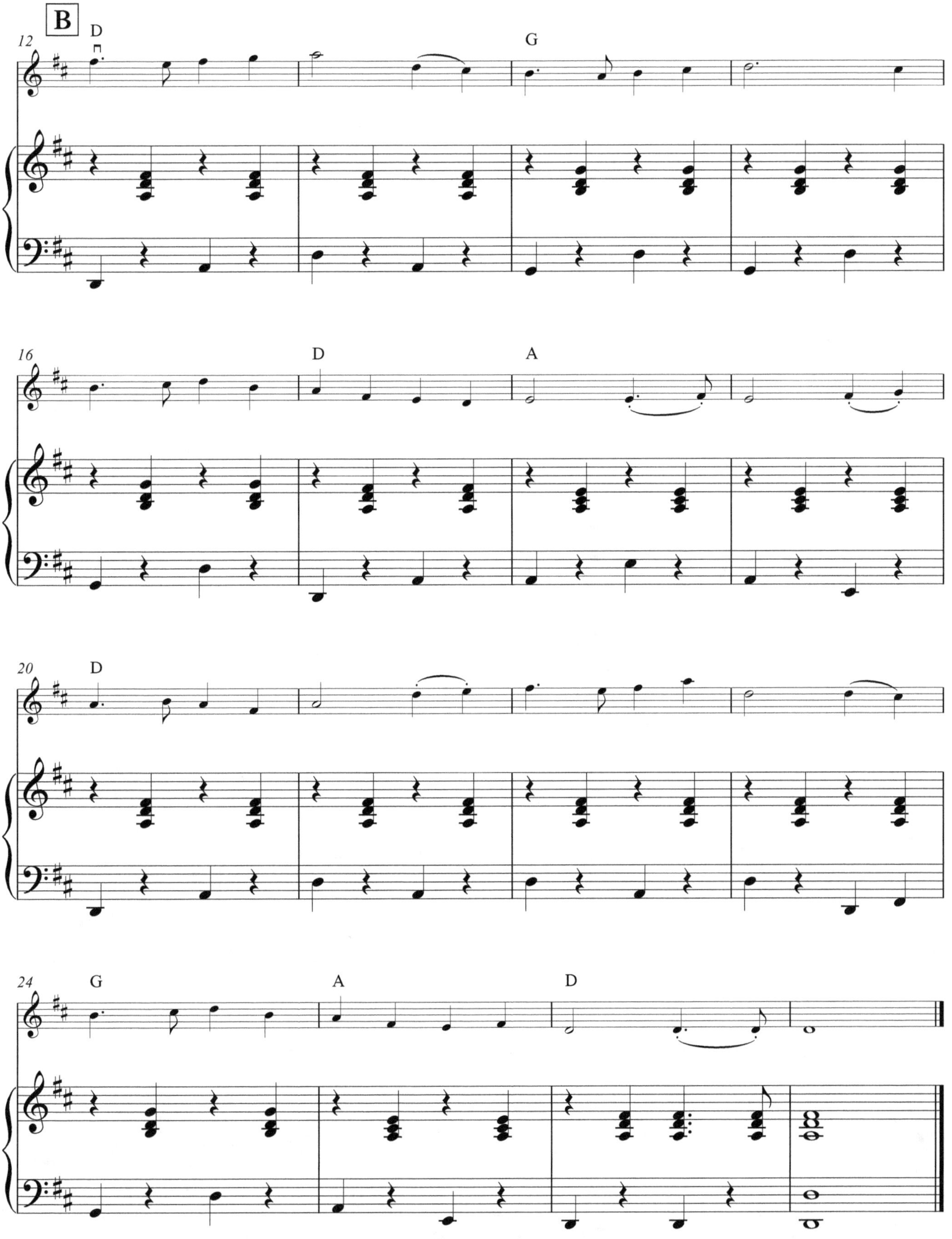
B
12
D
G
16
D
A
20
D
24
G
A
D

Si Bheag, Si Mhor

36

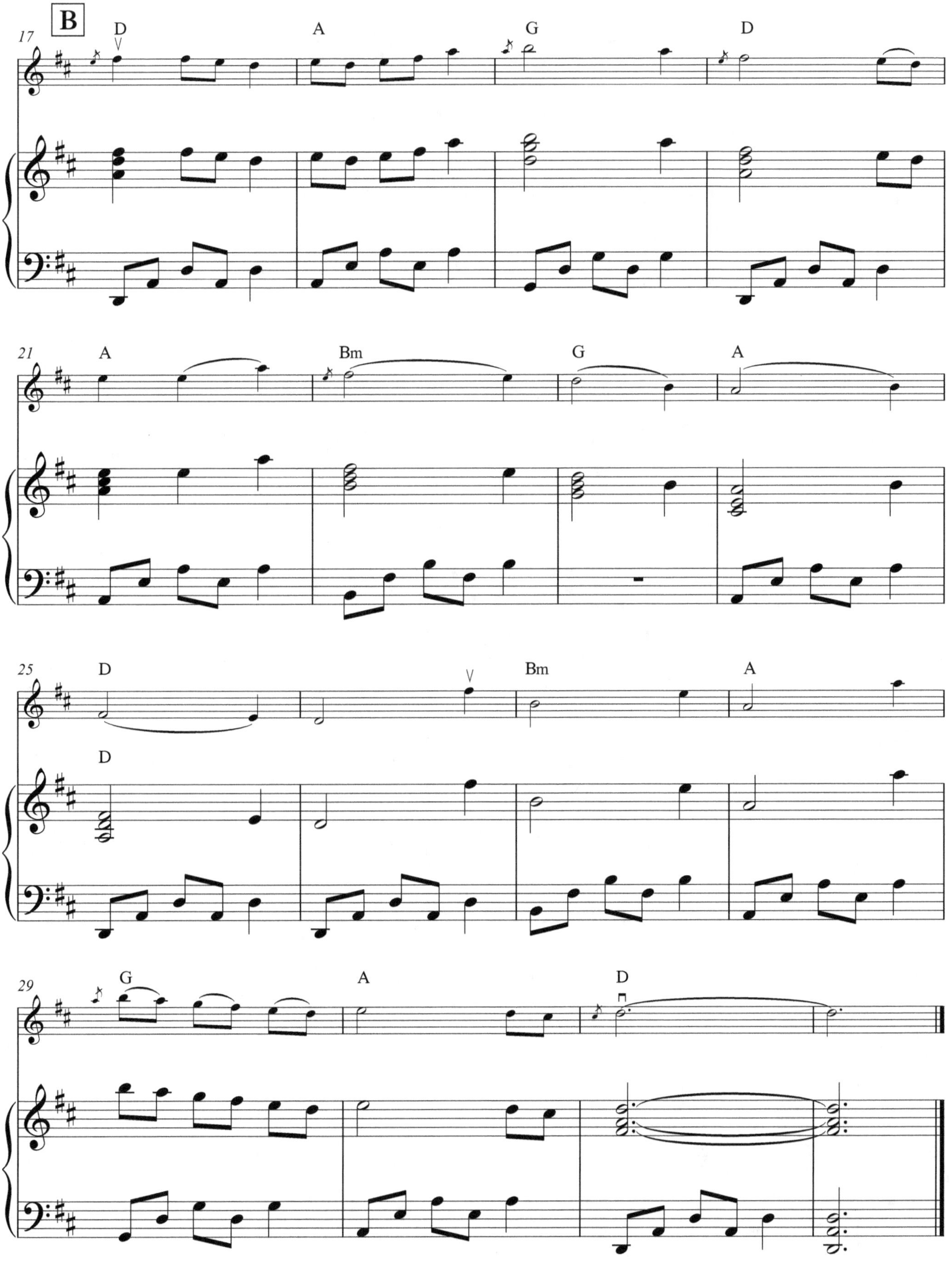
B
17
D
A
G
D
21
A
Bm
G
A
25
D
Bm
A
D
29
G
A
D

Acadian Two-Step

(For Two Fiddles)

38

St. Anne's Reel

(For Two Fiddles)

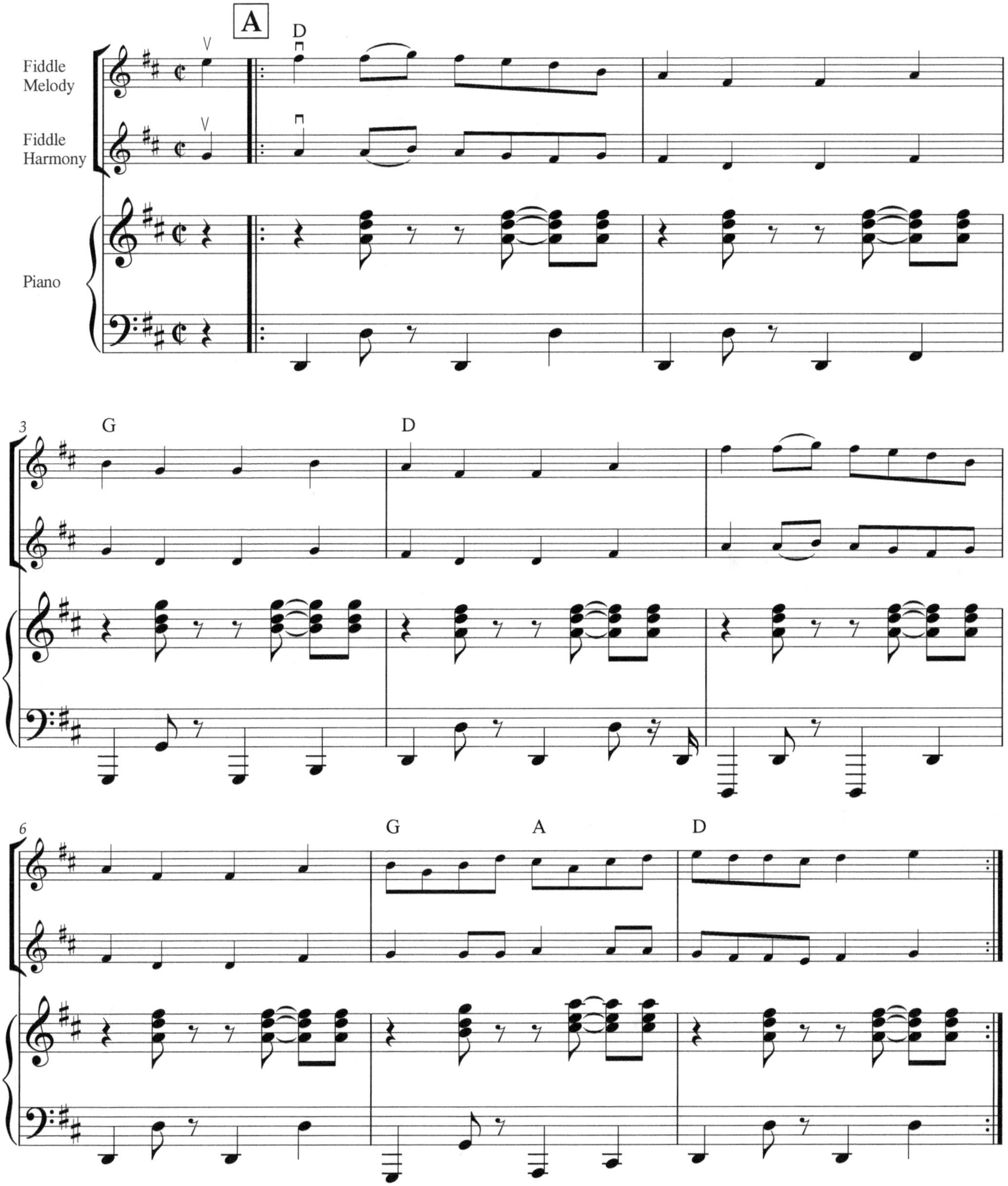

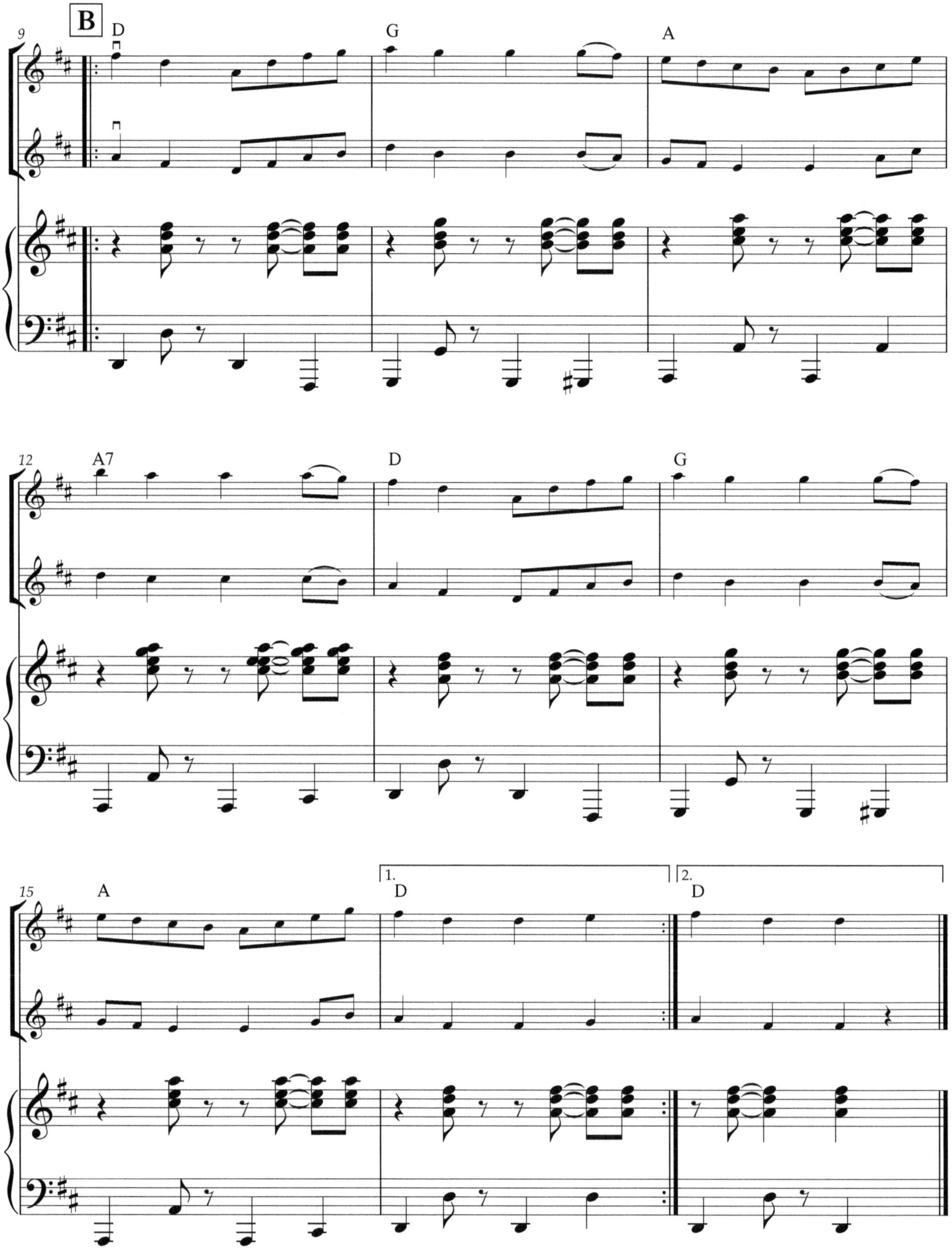
B
9
D
G
A
12
A7
D
G
15
A
1.
D
2.
D

Fire on the Mountain

Reel Saint-Antoine

Harvest Home

43

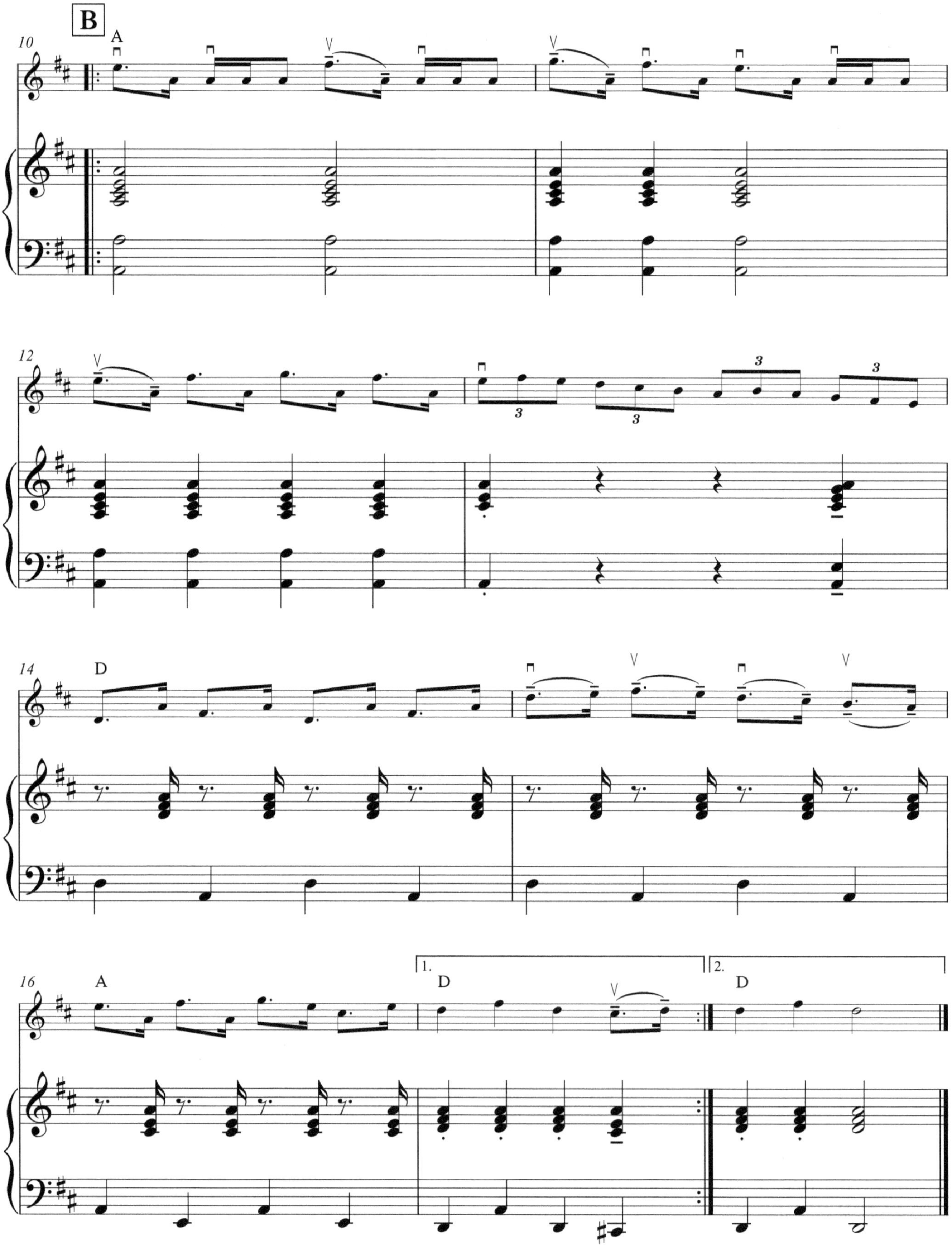
B
A
D
A
1.
D
2.
D

Irish Washerwoman

Shoes and Stockings

Kesh Jig

Doon the Brae

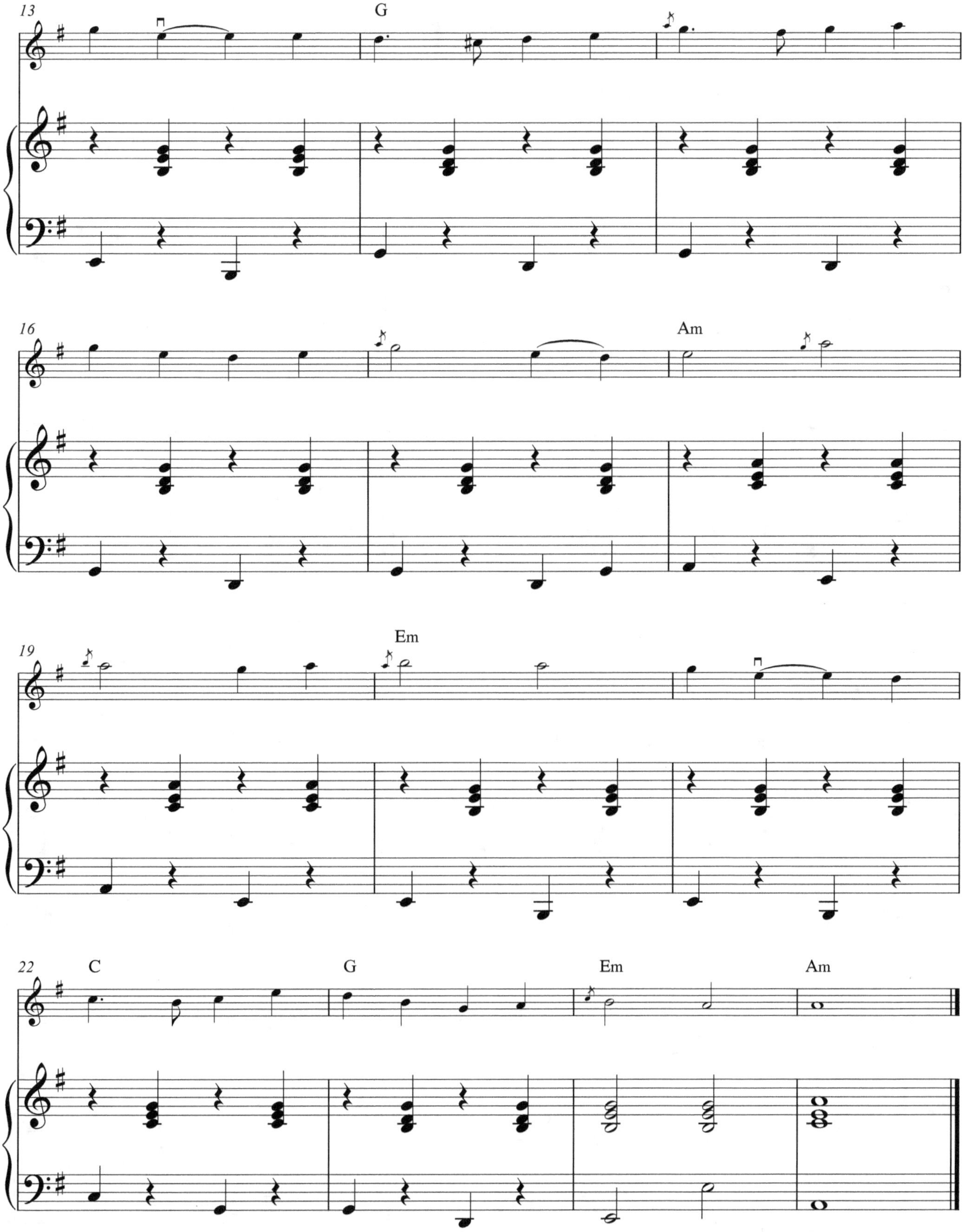
13
G
16
Am
19
Em
22
C
G
Em
Am

Cindy

50

Rørospols

51

Liberty

Chéticamp

53

Mairi's Wedding

Check out our other books in the *AltStrings Fiddle Method* series:

Books 3 and 4 build on your exciting skills, using lots of transcriptions of real recordings by today's great fiddlers!

Continue your study of playing accompaniment with chords, creating harmonies, and adding traditional ornamentation, by seeing for yourself how the masters do it!

Our series includes *AltStrings Fiddle Method* books for violin, viola, cello and bass.

Audio recordings and play-along backing tracks are available through iTunes as well as at *AltStrings.com*.

Check out *AltStrings.com* for sheet music arrangements of traditional, folk, pop, rock, jazz and holiday music, for over 20 types of bowed string ensemble!

Happy Fiddling!